Especially for
_____

From
_____

Date
_____

© 2011 by Barbour Publishing, Inc.

ISBN 978-1-61626-171-9

All rights reserved. No part of this publication may be reproduced or transmitted for commercial purposes, except for brief quotations in printed reviews, without written permission of the publisher.

Scripture taken from the HOLY BIBLE, NEW INTERNATIONAL VERSION®. NIV®. Copyright © 1973, 1978, 1984 by International Bible Society. Used by permission of Zondervan. All rights reserved.

Published by Barbour Publishing, Inc., P.O. Box 719, Uhrichsville, Ohio 44683, www.barbourbooks.com

Our mission is to publish and distribute inspirational products offering exceptional value and biblical encouragement to the masses.

Printed in China.

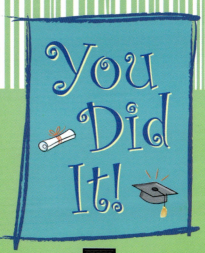

You've worked *hard* to reach this point. I've watched you grow and learn, and I am so proud of you. You did it!

Trust in the L<small>ORD</small> with all your heart and lean not on your own understanding;

in all your ways acknowledge him, and he will make your paths straight.

P<small>ROVERBS</small> 3:5–6

Always dream to shoot higher than you know how to. Don't bother just to be better than your contemporaries or predecessors. Try to be **better than yourself**.

WILLIAM FAULKNER

We can do anything we want if we stick to it long enough.

HELEN KELLER

What lies behind us and what lies before us are tiny matters compared to what lies within us.

RALPH WALDO EMERSON

Always remember:
Six months after graduation,
a good reputation will get you
farther than anything on
your résumé.

They can
conquer
who
believe
they can.

RALPH WALDO EMERSON

Have an optimistic attitude. Be positive.

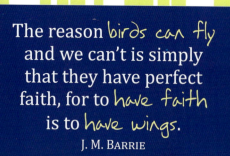

Do not follow where the path may lead. Go instead where there is no path and leave a trail.

RALPH WALDO EMERSON

A champion is someone who gets up even when he can't.

UNKNOWN

If a *caterpillar* refused to change, it could never become a *butterfly*. Trust God to give you wings.

FAITH STEWART

"Man looks at the outward appearance, but the LORD looks at the heart."

1 SAMUEL 16:7

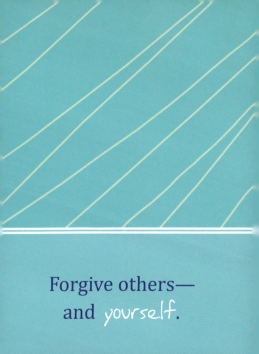

Forgive others—
and yourself.

There is nothing like a *dream* to create the future.

VICTOR HUGO

"I'm sorry" and "I blew it" make more friends than any explanation.

Life affords no greater pleasure than **overcoming obstacles**.

UNKNOWN

Do a little more each day than you think you possibly can.

LOWELL THOMAS

> A successful person is one who can lay a firm foundation with the bricks that others throw at him or her.
>
> DAVID BRINKLEY

The **value of life** lies not in the length of days, but in the use we **make** of them.

MICHEL DE MONTAIGNE

The world of tomorrow belongs to the person who has the vision today.

ROBERT SCHULLER

The best thing about the future is that it comes only one day at a time.
ABRAHAM LINCOLN

Success is to be **measured** not so much by the position that one has **reached** in life as by the obstacles which he has overcome trying to **succeed**.

BOOKER T. WASHINGTON

We find in life
exactly what
we put into it.

RALPH WALDO EMERSON

Knowledge is proud that it knows so much; wisdom is humble that it knows no more.

WILLIAM COWPER

There is no one you will ever meet who cannot **do something better** or see something more clearly than you can. Ask yourself every time you meet someone new, "What can I learn from this person?"

Every great *achievement* was once considered impossible.

UNKNOWN

Whatever you do, do it all for the glory of God.

1 Corinthians 10:31

Who stops being *better* stops being *good.*

OLIVER CROMWELL

Always be **first-rate** version of yourself, instead of a **second-rate** version of somebody else.

JUDY GARLAND

Without the Way there is no going; Without the Truth there is no knowing; Without the Life there is no living.

Thomas à Kempis

If you can *imagine* it,
you can *dream* it.
If you can dream it,
you can *become* it.

WILLIAM ARTHUR WARD

God knows the
secret plan
Of the things He will
do for the world,
Using your hand.

Toyohiko Kagawa

You are a part of the **great plan**, an indispensable part. You are needed; you have your own unique share in the *freedom* of Creation.

MADELEINE L'ENGLE

> Success is never a **destination**—
> it is a journey.
>
> SATENIG ST. MARIE

Spend more time with your friends and family. You will never regret it.

Those who hope in the LORD*. . .will* soar on wings *like eagles.*

ISAIAH 40:31

I cannot change the *whole world*, but I can change a small part of it.

Kay Florentino

I just want to do *God's will*. And He's allowed me to go **over the mountain**. And I've looked over, and I've seen the *Promised Land*.

Martin Luther King Jr.

> *May the God of hope fill you with all joy.*
>
> ROMANS 15:13

Never be afraid
to trust an unknown
future to a known God.

CORRIE TEN BOOM

I don't know what *your destiny* will be, but one thing I know: the only ones among you who will be really *happy* are those who sought and found how to serve.

DR. ALBERT SCHWEITZER

Self-confidence is the first requisite to great undertakings.

DR. SAMUEL JOHNSON

Work at something you enjoy—something that's **worthy** of your time and **talent**.

Be generous
with your time,
your money,
your attention.
You won't be sorry.

Start every day by giving your heavenly Father a **thank-you** for simply being alive.

Veni, Vidi, Vici.
I came.
I saw.
I conquered.
JULIUS CAESAR

This above all:
To thine own
self be true.
WILLIAM SHAKESPEARE

We *must believe* we are gifted for something, and that this thing, at *whatever cost,* must be attained.

MADAME CURIE

Forgetting what is behind and straining toward what is ahead, I press on toward the goal to win the prize for which God has called me.

PHILIPPIANS 3:13–14

Nothing great was ever achieved without *enthusiasm*.

RALPH WALDO EMERSON

Each man is given
a bag of tools,
A shapeless mass,
a book of rules;
And each must make—
ere life is flown—
A stumbling block or a
stepping-stone.

R. L. Sharpe

The **secret of success** is the constancy of *purpose*.

BENJAMIN DISRAELI

Be **decisive**. Don't be afraid to be wrong. We all make mistakes, but you'll never *accomplish* anything if you never act at all.

When love and skill **work together**, expect a masterpiece.

JOHN RUSKIN

When I am delivering my very best, that is when *I feel successful.*

— Art Fettig

Your word *is a lamp to my feet and a light for* my path.

Psalm 119:105

Use what *talents* you possess; the woods would be very silent if no *birds sang* except those that *sang best*.

HENRY VAN DYKE

Commit yourself
to getting better
and better at
whatever you do.

> The **secret** of *happiness* is not in doing what **one likes** but in liking what one *has to do.*
>
> J. M. Barrie

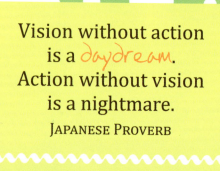

The poor man is not he who is without a cent, but he who is *without a dream.*

HARRY KEMP

Faith is deliberate **confidence** in the character of God whose ways you may not **understand** all the time.

OSWALD CHAMBERS

There are two ways to **live your life**. One is as though nothing is a *miracle*. The other is as though *everything is a miracle*.

ALBERT EINSTEIN

The future belongs to those who *believe* in the *beauty* of their *dreams.*

ELEANOR ROOSEVELT

Find your **joy in God** and others rather than in possessions.

Be content with your surroundings but not with *yourself* till you have made the **most of them**.

Unknown

Let us run with perseverance *the race marked out for us.*

HEBREWS 12:1

Two roads in a wood and I—
I took the one less
traveled by,
And that has made all
the difference.

Robert Frost

Dare to *dream big* dreams and then wait on God.

ELLYN SANNA

Don't aim for **success** if you want it; just do what you love and **believe** in, and it will come **naturally**.

D‌AVID F‌ROST

If you ever find *happiness* by hunting for it, you will find it as the old woman did her lost spectacles, **safe on her own** nose all the time.

Josh Billings

This shall be my parting word: Know what you want to do—*then do it!*

ERNESTINE SCHUMANN-HEINK